When You Need A Timeout

When You Need A Timeout

Create the Ultimate Stress-Free Getaway
One Relaxing Day at a Time

DR. BARBARA MITCHELL, DCH

Visit Dr. Barbara's website at:
www.thecalmingbreath.com

Copyright © 2008 by Barbara Mitchell

All rights reserved. No part of this publication may be reproduced, stored in a retrieval system or transmitted, in any form, or by any means, electronic, mechanical, recorded, photocopied, or otherwise, without the prior permission of the copyright owner, except by a reviewer who may quote brief passages in a review.

ISBN: 978-0-9820209-0-6

Library of Congress Control Number is 2008909519

Printed in the United States of America

Contents

Acknowledgments	....	9
Introduction	....	11
PART ONE	Take a Deep Breath	15
Chapter One	Stressssed...	17
Chapter Two	Let's Talk About Stress…	21
	Can You Handle That?	22
Chapter Three	Waiting to Exhale.................................	25
	Take a Deep Breath..............................	26
Chapter Four	Start Living Your Dream Today	29
	First Find Your Passion.........................	30
Chapter Five	Excite Your Senses	37
	Sit Back, Relax and Enjoy the Show	38
	Capture Your Joy..................................	39
PART TWO	This Time Is For You: Mind, Body and Spirit	45
Chapter Six	Don't Worry, Be Happy........................	47
	Quiet Joy Every Morning......................	48
	The Keys to Happiness..........................	49

Chapter Seven	Twenty-Four Little Hours:	
	It's "Go" Time	53
	The Night Before: "Me" Time	54
	Free Your Mind and the "Best"	
	Will Follow	54
	Free Your Mind/Body/Spirit	55
	On a Clear Day You Can See Forever	58
Chapter Eight	Body Flow: Nourish Your Body	61
	Food Talk	61
Chapter Nine	Create a Spa Experience	
	at Home-Soothe Your Spirit	65
	The Spa Bath	65
	Progressive Relaxation	66
PART THREE	Creative Escapes: The Art of Relaxation	69
Chapter Ten	Living the Life You Love	71
	Be in the Moment	71
	Positive Thoughts	72
	Have A Great Day From	
	Morning Till Night!	74
	Breathe In Energy	76
Chapter Eleven	If You Want My Body	81
	Soothing Spa Treatments	81
Chapter Twelve	Let's Get Physical	87
	Popular Alternative Therapies	88

PART FOUR	*What a Difference a Day Makes*	91
Chapter Thirteen	*It's Time to Call It a Day*	93
Chapter Fourteen	*Self-Discovery—*	
	There's Joy in Being Me	97
	Life Is What You Make It	99
Chapter Fifteen	*There's Always Something*	103
	I've Got a New Attitude	103
Chapter Sixteen	*Live Your Life*	111
	A New Way of Being	112
	Be Good to Yourself—You Deserve It	112
About The Author		117

Acknowledgments

Thank you Fred, my super spouse, for supporting my vision for this book, encouraging me through bouts of writer's block with your insightful suggestions and patiently reading and re-reading my drafts.

Thank you too, Kim, my delightful daughter, for always reminding me that the best way to convey my vision to the reader is to assume nothing and explain everything.

I love you both, always.

Introduction

*H*aven't you sometimes felt so overwhelmed, so tired of it all that you fantasized, "What would it feel like to just walk away from my responsibilities, worries, stress—just for a little while? Yes. Let the spouse, children, parents, siblings, relationships, job, etc., fend for themselves for once. I need a break!"

According to the American Psychological Association, one-third of Americans are living with extreme stress. You may be one of those who have not even realized the mental and physical toll that day-to-day stress is taking. However, the detrimental effects on your health are well documented. The irritability, depression, heart palpitations, fatigue, compulsive eating, unexplained anxiety, insomnia and body aches and pains you sometimes feel are all signs of a body and mind under stress.

When You Need a Timeout will show you how a one-day getaway, twenty-four hours of carefree, worry-free, tension-free time away—just for you—can make a big difference in reducing the stress in your life. This is an action plan with self-reflective exercises that address the emotional, physical and planning needs that must be satisfied before you can get away *without feeling guilty*. These self-help exercises will help you take charge of your life.

Introduction

This how-to guide is chock-full of tips and techniques that demonstrate how to really relieve your stress, guilt, fears and any other emotional baggage you bring to the table. It shows you how to absolve yourself from past wrongs through compassionate forgiveness and provides techniques to recapture the excitement of your childhood dreams and help you relive your happiest memories.

Finally, *When You Need a Timeout* shows you how to manage your day-to-day stress by introducing you to the art of relaxation. You'll learn how to pamper and nurture yourself on a daily basis…even when no one else will.

Think about this: If you had only twenty-four hours to live your life, how would you live it? Doing something you're passionate about? Recapturing your *joie de vivre*? That is what this book is about. Be prepared to enjoy a fun and sometimes inspirational journey along the way—from imagining to living your ultimate one-day getaway.

This book is dedicated to you, for those days *When You Need a Timeout*.

"Every person deserves a day away
in which no problems are confronted,
no solutions searched for."
—Maya Angelou

PART ONE

Take a Deep Breath

Chapter One

Stressssed.....

You Know Who You Are:

YOU'RE Cassidy,* the newlywed, educated, ambitious career woman. Your hard work and study of role models are beginning to pay off. You've begun to master the art of office politics, gotten on committees with the people you wish to impress and are on an upwardly mobile job track. But your spouse wants a child. You don't. Not now, anyway. As a result, you're having a lot of arguments at home. There's a lot of tension, and the stress is wearing you down. Lately you've begun to question the health of your marriage.

You're **Dawn**, the over-anxious, always exhausted single parent. The responsibility of being both mother and father to two children—disciplining, problem solving, worrying about their well-being—is overwhelming at times. Add to that the tension and frayed nerves caused by a thankless job and an insensitive boss. And all that stress is making you fat, because food—and plenty of it—is the only thing providing solace. But you can't stand the way you look with all that extra weight. Your stress level is over the top. Sometimes you just want to scream! You've got to find some down time…some "me time" just for you.

You're **Jennifer,** the overextended, multitasking wife and soccer mom. But the children need you less and less, and you're anxiously wondering how to fill the void. You're nervous about your appearance—you may have "let yourself go" a little over the years. You question your husband's fidelity even though he's given you no reason to. Your job skills are rusty, and the thought of interviewing scares you to death. Besides, you don't have a college degree. What kind of work can you do? Most disturbing, you've gotten into the habit of having a few glasses of wine every night, and you're worried you may be drinking too much.

You're **Nicole,** the successful, high-powered career woman with no time for or interest in a private life. Until now. There's a nagging health issue you need to address, but you have avoided seeing a doctor for fear that the diagnosis might spin your world out of control. You used to be proud of your independent "I can take care of myself" attitude. But if you have to take time off to recuperate, there's no one you can turn to for help with your emotional and physical well-being. And while you live comfortably, everything you have is on your shoulders. If—worst-case scenario—this is an illness requiring a long recuperation period, what resources do you have to depend on? This is keeping you up nights, and insomnia has become your nightly companion.

You're **Julia,** divorced, one of the "sandwich generation." Your adult child has come back to live at home, and your aging parents need more and more of your time and resources. You're fatigued all the time and emotionally drained from caring for two generations of loved ones. The weight of having all the decision-making fall on your shoulders—some of it crucial when it comes to your parents' future needs—is making you frustrated and irritable. You walk a thin line between helping your child get on his feet financially (and emotionally) and trying to encourage more maturity and effort on his part to show independence and move out. Your parents cannot live alone too much longer, but you're not ready to shoulder the burden of full-time caregiver if they move in with you. It's not just the finances—although right now you don't know where the money will come from. But lately old wounds keep opening up when the three of you spend time together. You need to clear the air—find your voice—before you again become the timid child in this new parent/adult-child arrangement.

You're **Toni**, a perky, energetic widow looking forward to early retirement. After years of hard work, you're envisioning a life of leisure: indulging in your favorite hobbies, maybe doing some volunteer work and traveling to exotic places with your group of gal pals. That was the plan up until a year ago. That was when you learned your pension wouldn't cover your townhouse mortgage. And only barely cover your everyday living expenses. Your chronic worries over finances have reduced a once-sunny, "happy to be alive" person to one who experiences long periods of moping and mild depression. Except for the days you *have* to get up for work, you spend most of the day in bed; lacking the energy or interest to even get dressed. To compound your belief that "one thing after another goes wrong," your checkup revealed you have osteopenia—one step closer to osteoporosis. That's the last straw. On top of being financially strapped, you now have illness and infirmity to look forward to in your senior years.

Take a Timeout

You may have been living under stress for so long now that your headaches, stomach upsets, tense muscles, clenched teeth and short temper have become second nature. But something inside you is clearly not happy with the status quo. You're ready to make a change, to feel better about yourself, to live a more supportive lifestyle. You're ready to take a timeout. You need a getaway from stress in order to recharge and retune your life.

---

*The profile vignettes are based on true-life stories; the names of real people have been changed.

Chapter Two

Let's Talk About Stress...

Did You Know:

1. Our bodies give us signs that we are under stress—irritability, depression, heart palpitations, fatigue, compulsive eating, unexplained anxiety, insomnia and body aches and pains.
2. Sources of stress are found in the environment (noise, pollution, world events); our personal lives (work, family, relationships, peer pressure, finances, social events, deadlines); our physical health (illness, poor nutrition, aging, injury, lack of exercise); and our thoughts (negative emotions—anger, guilt, grief, trauma and obsessive thoughts).
3. Not all stress is negative. A new home, job promotion, new baby and new relationships are all examples of positive stress. Stress becomes a negative event when the situation appears dangerous, painful or unfair and we don't have the resources to cope. Too many negative events experienced over a long period of time can result

in a compromised immune system and subsequent health problems.
4. Five keys to managing stress: (1) Practice physical and mental relaxation techniques; (2) eat a healthful diet rich in fruits, vegetables, lean meats and whole grains; (3) drink plenty of water; (4) exercise regularly; (5) laugh often.
5. Self-hypnosis is an excellent technique for alleviating stress-related conditions such as headaches, insomnia, nervous tics, nail-biting, anxiety and high blood pressure.
6. Meditation, visualization and deep breathing are relaxation techniques that help the body recover physically and emotionally from the harmful effects of stress.

CAN YOU HANDLE THAT?

Some people see stress as a challenge and take it in stride. Others may become overwhelmed and end up physical wrecks. It's helpful to understand exactly how you handle stress. Are you making yourself more vulnerable because your coping strategies are less than resourceful? Below is a list of some common ways people cope when faced with stressful situations. You'll recognize a few of them from the profiles of Cassidy, Dawn, Jennifer, Nicole, Julia and Toni.

Check all that apply to you.

When Under Stress:

1. _____ I withdraw emotionally and do nothing.
2. _____ I confront the problem and work to resolve it.
3. _____ I eat or sleep more than I should.
4. _____ I engage in physical activity to "blow off" the pressure.
5. _____ I drink and/or smoke too much.

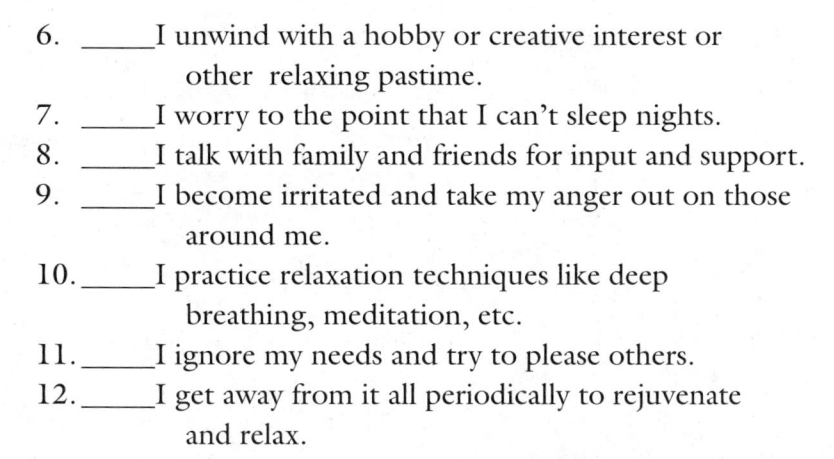

6. _____I unwind with a hobby or creative interest or other relaxing pastime.
7. _____I worry to the point that I can't sleep nights.
8. _____I talk with family and friends for input and support.
9. _____I become irritated and take my anger out on those around me.
10. _____I practice relaxation techniques like deep breathing, meditation, etc.
11. _____I ignore my needs and try to please others.
12. _____I get away from it all periodically to rejuvenate and relax.

Your Score: Did you check more of the even-numbered answers or more of the odd-numbered answers? The even-numbered answers represent the more constructive coping strategies. Take a look at the odd-numbered strategies you checked. Those are the areas you need to work on. Recognize them as opportunities to take charge of an aspect of your life that you're not handling to the best of your ability. Focus on what is possible, and set your sights on accomplishing it. Begin by drawing from the self-assertive (even-numbered) answers. Adapt those strategies to fit your specific needs. When you believe you are in control, you are better able to handle stressful situations. That's empowering. The lesson of this exercise: It is not the stress but the way you handle it that's most important to your physical and emotional health.

Chapter Three

Waiting to Exhale

*F*irst, let's try some techniques designed to relieve the stress you've been carrying. As you learned in the last chapter, stress is a fact of life, and not all stress is negative. Yet even positive events, like planning your wedding day, for example, can become overwhelmingly stressful if you don't have the resources to cope. And like the women profiled in the opening vignettes, you end up feeling pulled in so many directions at once that you don't know what to deal with first. You stay "geared up" and can't seem to relax. Sound a little like your life?

To make matters worse, recent research shows that too much stress can make you fat. When we are stressed, our bodies release the hormone cortisol, which is designed to give extra energy when we need it. But cortisol also increases blood sugar, which in turn increases our appetite for sugary and fattening treats, the comfort foods we turn to.

Dawn, the single parent, can attest to this. She's been caught up in this *stress = weight gain* loop for so long that any weight loss she achieves is short lived. Diets work in the short term (you name it, she's tried it) but inevitably she puts the weight back on, and then some. And since she hates to exercise, her weight-loss struggle is twice as hard. It's gotten so frustrating that Dawn is beginning to believe that, unlike most of the women in her family, she's the unlucky one who inherited the "fat" gene!

"Stress eating" can be a thing of the past once you learn simple relaxation methods to reduce stress. In fact, for all of the above reasons, it's obvious that some relaxation techniques and exercises should be added to your daily routine. Following are three that are easy and very effective:

Hint: Record these relaxation techniques and exercises so you can play back and listen to them as often as needed.

Take a Deep Breath...

Deep breathing is a tried-and-true way to relieve tension on the spot, especially when you are angry or nervous. Here's how:

Blow It Off:

1. Take a slow, deep breath through the nose.
2. Blow the air out through the mouth slowly and forcefully.
3. Continue points 1. and 2. until you begin to feel relaxed.
4. Give yourself an appropriate affirmation. For example, to relieve anger, you might say, "I'm calm and in control. I'm not going to let her/him get to me." If it's nervous tension, you might say, "I've done this successfully in the past. I'm going to be great giving this presentation!"

When nervousness or extreme tension cause us to take rapid, shallow breaths, **the calming breath** exercise forces us to breathe deeply. This deep-breathing exercise rapidly brings oxygen to the cells, soothes the nervous system, relaxes the muscles and slows a racing heart:

The Calming Breath:

1. Close your eyes and focus your awareness on your breathing.
2. Exhale toxic air, inhale cleansing air…slowly…easily, in and out.
3. Place your hand softly on your stomach and observe its rise and fall in concert with your breathing.
4. Allow the calmness of the breath to calm your mind.
5. Next, take deep, slow abdominal breaths through the nose to the count of six, then exhale through the mouth to the count of nine.
6. As you exhale slowly, mentally say the word "relax."
7. Continue your slow, deep abdominal breathing until you begin to feel relaxation flow to each part of your body. Breath and thoughts quiet…peaceful.

Jennifer, the soccer mom, found that her stressful thoughts spiraled out of control throughout the day, especially when she was alone in the house. She needed a way to reduce her stress on the spot. **Self-hypnosis for relaxation** is a quick, easy-to-learn exercise that dissolves tension immediately. With some practice, Jennifer found this technique to be more effective than drinking a glass of wine. Not only was self-hypnosis immediately relaxing, Jennifer also began to feel relief from the daily tension headaches she'd been experiencing.

Self-Hypnosis for Relaxation:

1. Touch your thumb to your forefinger, making an "OK" circle.
2. Beginning on the exhalation, take three slow, deep breaths through the nose.
3. On the last exhalation, gently close your eyes and repeat a word or phrase opposite your problem, i.e., "I am calm and relaxed" to counter tension or anxiety.
4. Focus on your slow, deep, rhythmic breathing.
5. Now think of your favorite color, sound or special memory.
6. Allow the good feelings and sensations from this imagery to envelope you.
7. Find a positive word such as peace, love or happiness to describe these feelings.
8. Next, mentally repeat your positive word to increase the enjoyment of this peaceful, relaxing experience.
9. Then, when you are ready, slowly count from one to five.
10. Open your eyes…feeling refreshed and deeply relaxed.

Chapter Four

Start Living Your Dream Today

Suppose I made you this offer. I will show you how to take one day that will add meaning to your life, not take away from it. I will show you how to live a day with no responsibilities, no worries. A carefree day. A day to take pause and explore what's important in your life. You will spend this day doing anything your heart desires. Rediscovering what you once loved. Reliving the happiest moments in your life. You'll get to do only those things you have a passion for. Do only those things that bring you joy and pleasure. Live out your dreams! All I ask in return is that you *promise* to spend the entire day on you, doing wonderful things for you, just you and only you.

Would you accept my offer? Don't let the moment pass. If your answer is **yes**, then sign here_____. There's no time like the present to start living your dream of a stress-free getaway day.

First Find Your Passion

Start by visualizing your goal. What would you do with this day? How would you spend it? Ask yourself, "What would bring me joy and pleasure? What am I passionate about? What would I do with this precious twenty-four hours all to myself? What do I want to do so badly, I'd do just that?" Grab a pen and paper, and begin mapping your journey. Create a wish list of activities that you know you would enjoy. You know, those activities you've had to put off so far because, well, you haven't had the time to think of yourself. Because life's too hectic! There were too many others to please. So all you did was dream that one day you'd find the time to do them.

Be sure to list those activities that you always wanted to do but were afraid to try. Give your inner child free rein. This is your opportunity to record your wildest dreams and fantasies. Even a "scary" activity can become an "exciting" activity, depending on the self talk you use to describe it. Both variations give you a heart-pumping adrenaline rush, but the internal representation—the way you feel about them—is different. If you want to give serious consideration to an activity in this scenario you have to change how you represent it to yourself. In other words, change what the activity means to you, then you'll be able to change its effect on you.

Reframe It:

Start by accepting your fear of the "scary" activity, but be determined to try it anyway. For example, let's suppose you enjoy spirited debates with your friends but are petrified at the thought of giving a speech before an audience. What are you going to do when your boss asks you to make the opening remarks at the next public meeting? Before you give that talk, you will have to change the way you perceive public speaking. A technique called

reframing enables you to literally change the way you see, hear, think about and respond to any situation. By using different words to describe the event (content), or by changing the event to one in which you have more of an advantage (context), you can change your emotional response. Let's see how **reframing** works for the above example:

1. Begin by jotting down the words that describe what you're feeling when you think of the exciting activity—list them under the heading "Spirited Debates With Friends" in column one.
2. Then, under the heading "Speaking in Front of an Audience," list the words that describe your feelings toward the "scary" event in column two.
3. Compare the two lists and note the words you've used to describe each activity. Observe the words you use when you feel afraid versus the ones you use when feeling excited.
4. Revise the lists. Begin by moving the empowering words from column one ("Spirited Debates") into column two ("Speaking in Front of an Audience"). For example, if you feel *enthusiastic*, *spontaneous* and *self-assured* when making points to friends—move those words to the public-speaking column. Remember, your visceral reaction to the stressful situation is the same as to the "exciting" one. Your muscles will still tense, your heart rate, blood pressure and breathing will increase, and you may still get a knot in your stomach.
5. Read the revised list out loud. Say relevant affirmations like "I love a challenge!" "I believe in my ability to succeed," "I can handle anything today," and "Today I will do this!" every time you read an empowering word on your "Speaking" list.
6. Record and play back your speech. Develop your sensory

acuity for voice and inflection. Decide where to adjust voice tempo or volume to make key points.
7. Close your eyes and imagine your favorite actor making your speech. Step into his or her body, become one as you master the role. Then rehearse out loud in front of a mirror, and develop your sensory acuity for body movement and projecting confidence.
8. Learn all you can about presentation skills, and study exceptional communicators to build more confidence.
9. List all the positive reasons you can think of to try it. Be upbeat.
10. Then be determined to do it!

So, the next time you have no choice but to do something difficult, try **reframing** it—and see how different you feel.

REFRAMING EXERCISE

Dislike	**Like**	**Desired Outcome**
Public Speaking	Friendly Debate	Public Speaking
I feel	I feel	I feel (reframed)
Petrified	Enthusiastic	Enthusiastic
Tongue-tied	Self-assured	Self-assured
Can't think	Spontaneous	Spontaneous
Tense	Relaxed	Relaxed
Faint	On Fire	On Fire

YOUR TURN

Dislike	**Like**	**Desired Outcome**
_____	_____	_____
I feel	I feel	I feel (reframed)
_____	_____	_____
_____	_____	_____
_____	_____	_____
_____	_____	_____

Now back to your **wish list.** Embrace your adventurous side! Just remember, this is a wish list of activities you would want to spend a day indulging in. Make it something you look forward to doing. Keep the spirit upbeat, and just enjoy the process!

MY WISH LIST

_____

_____

_____

_____

_____

_____

_____

_____

_____

_____

_____

_____

When You Need A Timeout

Chapter Five

Excite Your Senses

Now comes the fun part. You are about to take a "mini" vacation—a guided tour of your "what would make me happy" scenario. For this, let's try a visualization exercise to excite your senses. Just sit back, relax and enjoy the next few minutes.

Close your eyes. Take three deep, slow breaths. Inhale and exhale through your nose. Focus on your breathing—natural, rhythmic, effortless. Begin to think back to those times when you were very happy, very contented. When was one of the happiest times in your life? What were you doing? Vacationing on a tropical island? Skiing down a mountain slope? Winning an award or other recognition? How about enjoying a sunset or holding a child? Where were you…who were you with? Your first true love?

Maybe it's none of the above? Then fantasize! What would you like to be doing? The sky's the limit! This is **your** wish list! Your happiest times could be nothing more than relaxing all day with a good book; seeing back-to-back movies; visiting a museum or art gallery, pampering yourself all day at a spa. Or perhaps you're a little more ambitious. You might start that novel you always wanted to write; take a painting class, a singing lesson, a boxing lesson; learn to windsurf or ride a motorcycle. Or maybe you'd like to revisit a hobby or sport you once enjoyed…recapture a long-forgotten youthful dream or a talent you haven't nurtured. Did you always want to learn another language, prepare a gourmet meal, try an unusual exercise like tai chi, Pilates, yoga, belly dancing? Or dance the night away like you did back in the day? Remember, the sky's the limit. You name it, you dream it. Or go back in your mind and remember it.

Sit Back, Relax and Enjoy the Show

Are you there yet? In the movie of your mind? Imagining the moment? Notice the colors, sounds, smells, season of the year. Is the picture in your mind large, small, dark, bright, in color? A still life or a motion picture? Are you alone, with someone or in a crowd? Are there familiar sounds, voices, music, birds singing, waves crashing? Is the wind blowing? Does the air smell fresh, of flowers, damp from the ocean or like grandma's fresh-baked cookies? What can you taste? Is it cold, hot, wet, smooth, crunchy, sweet, tart, bitter? Is touch involved? How does it feel against your skin? Soft, hard, smooth, sharp, sensual? What kind of feeling does it invoke? Happiness, joy, delight, pride, melancholy, longing, warmth, comfort, love?

Visualize It:

Employ all your senses to make your fantasy come to life. See/feel/imagine every detail. Then, when you have the picture just the way you want it, make it life size and imagine yourself stepping right into it. Enjoy the experience as if you were right there—in the moment. Stay as long as you like. Then, when you are ready to come back to reality, take a deep breath and open your eyes.

You can enjoy this wonderful experience anytime you want

in the future. The technique is called **visualization**, and it is accomplished by creating mental impressions of your daydreams, memories and inner talk. The procedure, in seven simple steps:

Visualization:

1. Take slow, deep, rhythmic breaths. Focus on your breathing, the rise and fall of your chest.
2. Close your eyes and imagine your favorite person, place or event. Concentrate on making the image real—sharpen the picture.
3. See/imagine the sights, shapes and colors. Feel the air, moisture or textures on your skin. Listen to the sounds. Smell the aromas. Taste the foods. Make every detail real.
4. Enlarge the visual to life size.
5. Imagine yourself walking into this life-size image—your retreat, your haven.
6. When you feel nourished, enjoyed all that you want at this time, smile and remind yourself that you can enjoy this experience again anytime you want.
7. Take a deep breath, and open your eyes.

CAPTURE YOUR JOY

Now you know what your goal is. It is to capture that joy you once knew and relive it for a day. Get out your wish list now. Begin to refine it, eliminating those items that are physically impossible. But be creative. For example, you wish to sail around the world on a luxury cruise ship. But you don't have that kind of money or vacation time. Besides, it's not doable in twenty-four hours anyway. However, you could take one of the popular lunch or dinner cruises. You could even charter a private boat and dock at a secluded island for lunch. Or you could attend a travel show and immerse yourself in the seminars, videos and travel tips given by experts of exotic vacation destinations. One travel agency recently offered "A Night of Tuscany, Villas and Wine Tasting" to the public. Attend this event, and enjoy a wine-tasting excursion and a trip to another part of the world!

Suppose your fantasy is to be in a movie or television show. And you're looking to go a bit beyond a YouTube video? Well, you could find where and when a casting call for extras is being held—and show up for it. Or gather your courage and audition for a part in a community play. The atmosphere will be charged with the language and fervor of other amateur actors. You may not be selected for a role the first time around, but you'll be with like-minded artists who share your passion. So be persistent and plan to succeed!

The point is that even an impossible dream could have some elements that can be enjoyed in one day. There's a group of people somewhere doing exactly what you'd like to be doing. Your job is to find out how to make it happen. Do your research. Google it. Plan every aspect of your twenty-four-hour dream getaway.

For each item on your list ask yourself "why, where, when, how, with whom?" to further define what you need and what it is about that activity that gives you the most joy. In your research don't be afraid to ask someone with knowledge, expertise or resources who can help you with your decision.

Rework your list. Through the process of elimination a theme will begin to emerge. Think of a word that captures what you're feeling during this reverie. Go back and write that word at the top of your wish list. This is the feeling you want to recapture. Your *joie de vivre*—the joy you want to indulge in on your perfect day away. Which activity best represents it?

Revised Wish List

Theme: _____

_____

_____

_____

_____

_____

_____

_____

_____

_____

_____

When You Need A Timeout

Now that you know what you want to do, it's time to pick the day that you plan to make your "getaway"! Pick a day of the week that works for you. Clear your calendar. Arrange for babysitters, day-care services, in-house companions or help from relatives. Take a vacation day from work if you have to. Reserve a hotel room if you need it. Handle all these details well in advance to avoid any last-minute delays or disappointment.

PART TWO

*This Time Is For You:
Mind, Body and Spirit*

Chapter Six

Don't Worry, Be Happy

When you hear the song "Don't Worry, Be Happy" by Bobby McFerrin, does it put you in a good mood? Or do you find it irritating? It probably depends on what is going on in your life at the moment. The pursuit of happiness is highly individualistic. It has to do with your perceptions and beliefs about your quality of life. Does your life meet your idea of purpose and meaning, emotional connection, physical health? At the end of the day, being happy is about what is right for you.

The truth is, you have control over how you feel at any given moment. When you change how you think about a problem, you change how you feel. In an earlier chapter we talked about how to **reframe** the content and context of any event. The whole idea of that exercise was to learn how to release the emotional hold a problem may have over you. To break it down further, something happened in your past that subconsciously causes adverse feelings about the present problem. Its emotional hold, consequently, is based on past programming that may not support you in the present. So why hang on to feelings that no longer support you?

Make yourself a priority. In fact, you can do little things each day for a more fulfilling and enjoyable life. Begin by practicing one of the forms of relaxation outlined in this book. To start your day, don't just jump out of bed. Linger a moment to welcome the wonderful day to be…and give thanks. Add this simple ritual to start each day with quiet joy, positive thoughts and an attitude of gratitude:

> ## Quiet Joy Every Morning
>
> Every morning upon rising, take a moment to gaze out a window. Savor the joy of morning. Drink in the wonders of nature. Stop and allow yourself to be in awe…of the grandeur of the vast sky with its crisp dawn colors or muted grays…the changing patterns and faces in the clouds…the brilliance of the sunrise. Stay in this beautiful moment. Just feel. Let the feeling flow. Let it slowly flow.
>
> Now, have your gaze glide over the majestic trees…their distinct shapes…their patterned limbs and the sway of their leaves. Listen to the morning sounds…or quiet stillness: The morning hush. If a worry crosses your mind, say to yourself, "Not now. This is my moment, my time, my space, my peace of mind." Inhale slowly, deeply, to bring oxygen and energy flowing through your body. Exhale. Quiet Joy **Every** Morning.

The art of relaxation is a mindset, a belief that your body, mind and spirit deserve some downtime in order to recharge. And it doesn't have to cost you anything. You can give yourself small gifts of pleasure every day:

The Keys to Happiness

- **Greet** each day with a smile. When you wake up, greet the day with happy words: joy, zest, sunshine, glow, enjoyment.... Greet your loved ones with a smile and a "good morning." Each day is a brand-new opportunity to improve something in your life.
- **Visualize** beautiful memories. Remember the people, places and adventures you have known and loved. Transport yourself through quiet contemplation into those memories.
- **Replace** negative thinking with self-affirming thoughts. The next time you're beating yourself up—STOP. Instead, think of a compliment, thoughtfulness or a kind word someone gave you. Remember the times you coped with a difficult situation and succeeded. Learn the lesson. Move on.
- **Tell** someone you love them. Someone significant in your life—even yourself from time to time. Go ahead—make their day!
- **Lend** a helping hand. Do a kindness to others, and note how it warms your heart. That's your reward.
- **Share** laughs with family and friends. Laughter is the ultimate mood lifter. Do it often. Bask in the warmth of family and friends, and create new memories.
- **Be** at peace through faith, prayer, meditation or whatever way you connect to the Divine within you.
- **Do** something special just for you. This list is endless. Buy yourself flowers every week. Listen to music that puts you in a good mood. Get out and enjoy nature. Interact with a child. Create something with your hands. Pursue a goal. Buy something new. Get a massage. Meet a good friend for lunch. Etcetera...etcetera...etcetera.

So you see, you have the ability to find your own way of being happy. Before you know it, it will become who you are.

Nicole, the successful career woman, felt she had no reason to wake up happy. Although she didn't realize it at first, her anxiety about her health had her in a state of near depression. The slightest twinge or pain set her heart racing, and her thoughts focused on the worst-case scenario. She'd get an awful feeling in the pit of her stomach. Times like these found Nicole surfing the Internet, trying to match her symptoms to a disease. But trying to diagnose herself, she found, was a bad idea, as every symptom seemed connected to a myriad of illnesses. She knew she needed to get her life back but remained paralyzed in this loop of excessive worrying.

Nicole found that doing stress-reduction and relaxation exercises took her mind off her troubles temporarily. The more she practiced, the calmer and more centered her thoughts became. Her sense of panic, of feeling out of control, began to diminish. She found a space for release in her daily routine. She truly enjoyed and looked forward to this respite.

She began to focus on doing little things for herself that made her happy. For example, she loved fresh flowers—any kind, as long as they were yellow. She got into the habit of treating herself once a week to a small bouquet to put on her kitchen table. She rented comedies, watched sitcoms and even found herself watching cartoons! She needed to laugh more.

Eventually she found the confidence to do what she had to: make that doctor's appointment. Nicole was ready to get on with her life.

Toni, the energetic widow, knew she had to pull herself together. Those feelings of sadness, irritability and lack of energy were not at all like her. For quite some time she had been avoiding her friends. She was embarrassed by her change in fortune and had begun isolating herself. Last year they were all making plans to celebrate her retirement with a once-in-a-lifetime vacation in Hawaii. They had been pooling their money for quite some time to save for this big celebration. But when Toni found out she would have a tough time making ends meet on her pension, she needed a safety net. So she pulled her money out of the pool and placed it in a practical savings plan. But she felt she had let everybody down. Her friends now represented those happier times that she didn't want to be reminded of.

Of course her friends did not share her view. They had been trying for months, without success, to pull her out of her blues and get her interested in some favorite activities again. During one such phone conversation one of her friends asked with concern, "Tell me, how many hours pass in the day before you find your smile? When was the last time you had a good laugh?"

"Laugh?" Toni thought. "I don't even remember the last time I *smiled*." And with that thought, something shifted in her. She was fed up with moping around all day and feeling sorry for herself. Her catalyst for change was just that simple. From that day on Toni went into self-help mode. She knew it was time to give herself the gift of forgiveness. She did not go to bed without planning one small "pleasure" to look forward to the next day. She started each morning in the spirit of thankfulness and with the **Quiet Joy Every Morning** ritual. She started reaching out to family and friends again. Toni's healing had begun.

Chapter Seven

Twenty-Four Little Hours: It's "Go" Time

*A*T last, only twenty-four hours to go before your getaway. Gather everything you'll need for tomorrow. This might include "how to" videos, theater schedules, travel guides, hotel reservations, spa appointments, your copy of *When You Need a Timeout*, etc. You've told everyone who needs to know about your plans and arranged for all necessary sitters. You've scheduled a vacation day from work. Reserved a hotel room in advance. Packed your overnight bag, backpack and/or all necessities to ensure optimal enjoyment of your day away.

Plan to enjoy your own company this day. No family or friends (unless they play a role in your day-away experience). No phones, faxes, emails, clocks…no work of any kind. You will be spending the next twenty-four hours away from day-to-day worries. Twenty-four hours to yourself, to indulge yourself—and only yourself. Twenty-four hours to follow your heart's desires. Twenty-four hours that will recharge and renew you—body, mind and spirit.

Now here's the surprise! Your twenty-four hour ultimate getaway begins tonight.

The Night Before: "Me" Time

The night before your getaway has been set aside for "me" time—for serene self-reflection, self-discovery and quiet joy. Part Two of this book is devoted to helping you reach that peaceful mindset by resolving those weighty issues that have been causing you stress. Exercises for the mind, body and spirit are introduced now to ensure that your getaway tomorrow is carefree, worry free and guilt free. Since there's no time like the present, let's get started.

Free Your Mind and the "Best" Will Follow

Now it's time to deal with those weighty worries you've been carrying around. Decide now that any problems—be they financial or family, relationship, health or job related—will have to exist without you for a while. Promise to leave those burdens behind for *one* day. They'll be there, should you decide you want them back.

Freeing your mind from replaying painful emotions is a two-sided coin that takes into account pain inflicted *on you* as well as pain inflicted *by you*. You can accomplish this unburdening by following the **two-step process** below:

Step 1. Leave Your Worries on Your Doorstep

Sometimes an old emotional hurt will not die. You want to forget it and move on with your life, but the ill feelings just won't go away. This two-step **mind/body/spirit** exercise is designed to cleanse troubling thoughts once and for all:

FREE YOUR MIND/BODY/SPIRIT

Find a comfortable place to sit. Take three deep, slow breaths. Inhale and exhale through your nose. Focus on your even breathing—natural, rhythmic, effortless. Inhale deeply. Exhale slowly. Feel and sense the breaths flowing through both nostrils.

Gently close your eyes. Focus your awareness inward. Tune in to your inner stillness. Observe the quiet mind. If a worry should cross your mind, think about it briefly, then say to yourself, "I can handle it." Then turn your attention back to your breathing. Send the breath to any tightness in the body. Let go of the last bit of tension with slow, deep breaths. Relax now. It's tranquil in here…the problems of the world do not concern you right now…this is your time…your space…your chance for relaxation.

For a moment, imagine a big, fluffy cloud floating gently to earth. It looks very soft, and that calms and relaxes you. You reach out to touch it and, sure enough, a sense of peace surrounds you. And you decide to put all your worries in this cloud—all the heavy burdens you don't want to carry any longer. And you begin to feel lighter. Next you place all your pain, fear and frustration into the cloud. You begin to feel much lighter. Then you quickly toss all your anger, hurt, loneliness, guilt—and any other undesirable emotions, thoughts or actions you've been carrying—into the cloud. You no longer want or need them.

> When you've finished, say, "I release you…I let you go!" Then envision that cloud rising up, up, up towards the sun. And the closer the cloud gets to the sun, the smaller it becomes. Then the sun's rays shine through, a starburst of rainbow colors—bright reds, blues, greens, oranges, yellows and purples. And puff! All your troubles disintegrate. You feel lighter, like a huge weight has been lifted from your shoulders. You feel emotionally cleansed, totally at peace with yourself.
>
> Find your place of beautiful memories, something positive, something that makes you happy. And as the sun warms your body, feel that happiness begin to radiate from the depths of your being…up to your heart…to your throat…and find its way to a smile upon your lips. Decide now what you would like to take with you into your day—something of a positive, nurturing nature. Now open your eyes. Take a deep, cleansing breath. Your troubles are history. Free Your Mind/Body/Spirit.

Step 2. The Gift of Forgiveness

While relaxing, begin to think about forgiving someone—just for a day—toward whom you've harbored anger. Someone whom you've blamed for causing hurt, pain, embarrassment or guilt in your life. That someone is **you.** Think of all the negative things you say to and about yourself each day—"I'm not smart enough, not good enough. I'm too fat, skinny, dumb, ugly, tall, short. My nose is too big, my mouth too wide, my hair too straight, curly, kinky. My hips are too wide, my legs too thin, my feet too big…" and so on.

Although you've heard it before, it bears repeating: Nobody's perfect! Take a look around you. It seems everyone is getting "work" done these days. Face lifts, tummy tucks, liposuction. The cosmetics and plastic-surgery industry is a multi-billion-dollar testament to that. It's no secret that the pictures of models in magazines are airbrushed to create the illusion of perfection. "Insider secrets" to enhance your looks by changing what you wear or the way you walk, talk, etc., are everywhere. So if there's something you want to work on, you have options. Get gorgeous. Just don't go overboard trying to change your outward appearance. It's how you look inside that counts. That's where real change happens. And that's where a healthier outlook on life begins.

The point I'm making is this: We all have something about ourselves we'd like to change. But no matter how big the flaw, it's usually just cosmetic. Be grateful that you have that nose, hair, legs, etc., and that they function the way they should. Because in this world there is someone, somewhere without, who would gladly trade places with you.

Perhaps your negative self talk sounds something like this: "I should not have done or said that to him/her." "I wish I could take it back." "If I could go back and do it over again," etc. As for past events we wish we could change, the fact is that what could or should (or should not) have been done or said is irrelevant at this stage. The past has passed. We cannot physically go back in time and change it. It is done. Just recognize that you did the best you could based on your mental and emotional state at the time. Even in hindsight, and knowing what you know now, you may not have gotten different results.

For the sake of your own well-being, let go of self-recriminations. If you find that hard to do, use the power of your **mind** to change how you feel. Try this: Mentally relive the event but change the outcome to the way you would have liked it to be. Then visualize the event with the new outcome. Replay it *several* times in your mind. That's better, isn't it?

Resolve today to give yourself the gift of forgiveness. You've forgiven others many times in the past. Some for more egregious acts than your own. Isn't it time to bestow some of that compassion on you? Once you realize that suffering the distressing emotional consequences of past events no longer serves a purpose, you'll be free to move on. Take whatever you learned as a life lesson. Then vow to be good to yourself…you deserve it!

After practicing the steps in the **mind/body/spirit exercise**, **Julia**, sandwiched between elderly parents and adult child, became more willing to forgive old hurts remembered from childhood. Her anger dissolved with the understanding that her parents did the best they could with what they knew—which was based on their own strict "show no affection or emotions" upbringing. Julia symbolically severed the emotional ties of bad childhood memories and allowed the good memories to take their place. She was ready to move forward and relate to her parents in terms of the responsible adult she was. Subsequent conversations with her parents revealed that they desired to live independently as long as possible and not to move in with their daughter. What they needed from Julia was help contacting the agencies and coordinating the services they would need to remain independent. With this understanding, Julia felt as if a weight had been lifted from her shoulders. As a result of the more open communications, Julia now enjoys her family time more. And this she values above all else.

ON A CLEAR DAY YOU CAN SEE FOREVER

So now that your mind has been cleared of negative thoughts and responsibility, your getaway can be a relaxing and enjoyable experience. "Why is this mind/body/spirit clearing so important?" you might ask. Because you don't want any negative emotions or thoughts jumping out at you and spoiling your day.

Your getaway tomorrow is going to be a day of unadulterated joy. Nothing is allowed to interfere with or block your flow of positive energy tomorrow!

PROMISE: I promise to unconditionally forgive everyone who has hurt me, myself included, at least for one day.

Chapter Eight

Body Flow: Nourish Your Body

Plan to eat light, nutritious meals tomorrow to keep your energy up. Select portable, easy-to-carry foods if you're going to be on the go. Even if your ideal getaway includes white-glove service dining on a five-course gourmet meal at an upscale restaurant, a light, balanced breakfast will get you off to a good start.

FOOD TALK

We now know that certain foods and herbs have a calming effect on the body, while others have an antidepressant effect. Still other foods tend to create more stress. Cut back or eliminate substances known to aggravate anxiety and stress, such as caffeine, nicotine and stimulant drugs. Limit salt, sugar and alcohol consumption. Substitute with decaf and/or herbal ingredients whenever possible.

Increase your consumption of foods that boost your energy and lift your spirits. For example, blueberries, grapes, tomatoes and sweet potatoes are rich in stress-busting vitamin C; protein foods like skim milk and cottage cheese stabilize your blood sugar and help you feel less hungry; walnuts, asparagus and wild salmon help maintain levels of serotonin, the "feel-good" neurochemical in the brain.

It's easy to enjoy fresh, dried, frozen or vacuum-packed fruits, vegetables and whole-grain foods wherever your day takes you. Apples, oranges, bananas, cherry tomatoes, carrots, celery—just about any fruit or vegetable you enjoy will do. Raisins, yogurt, nuts, string cheese and granola bars are also no-fuss, portable, and easy to carry. They're all good, quick snacks. All are packed with important nutrients and carbohydrates, the body's preferred source for energy. As an added bonus for you weight watchers, most fruits and vegetables are naturally low in calories and fat.

You might want to start your day with whole-grain cereal mixed with fresh or dried fruit, whole-grain toast and a glass of pure fruit juice. Add a hard-boiled egg or piece of cheese for protein. Or have a fruit blender drink, or try a glass of tomato or vegetable juice. Add ice cubes made from grapefruit juice to a glass of pineapple juice. Or enjoy juicy fruits such as watermelon, oranges and grapes for a healthy start.

For lunch take advantage of salad bars or pre-cut salad mixes. Add soup and a hearty whole-grain sandwich to round out your meal. Include sautéed or steamed vegetables with your dinner entrée of grilled fish, chicken or steak.

Naturally you'll want to select foods you enjoy and are not allergic to. Drink plenty of water throughout the day to quench your thirst. Refresh and replenish with juice, juicy fruits and water-packed vegetables. In addition take along whatever vitamins and medication regimen you may be on.

Write out your menu for tomorrow. With the above in mind, select from a list of your favorite foods. And, yes, include that mouth-watering, decadent dessert. Eat it slooowly. Savor and enjoy every mouthful. That's one of those little rewards you can give yourself. Skip the guilt for a day.

TOMORROW'S MENU

Breakfast _____

_____

_____

_____

_____

_____

Lunch _____

_____

_____

_____

_____

When You Need A Timeout

Dinner _____

_____

_____

_____

_____

_____

Decadent Dessert _____

Chapter Nine

Create a Spa Experience at Home-Soothe Your Spirit

*P*lan to go to bed early tonight. Fresh sheets and pillowcases, please (satin sheets aren't bad either). A spray of lavender or a lavender sachet placed under the pillow will help ensure a restful night's sleep. Turn off the cell phone.

THE SPA BATH

But first, treat yourself to a luxurious spa bath. You're worth it. A hot bath is great for relaxing sore muscles. Have on hand all of the herbal oils, bath bubbles, fragrant soaps and powders you love. Choose such fragrances as lavender or lemongrass for their soothing properties. Their scent works as soon as you put them into the tub and breathe in. Soak large cotton pads in cooled chamomile tea for a soothing eye compress. Place a glass of water with a slice of lemon nearby to rehydrate after your soak. Light some scented candles. Put on soft, relaxing or romantic music. Slip into the tub. Place the cotton pads over your tired eyes. Lay your head on a bath pillow or rolled-up towel. Take a slow, deep breath while you practice head-to-toe **progressive relaxation**.

Progressive relaxation involves tensing and releasing the large muscle groups of the body. If physically tightening and releasing your muscles is impractical, an effective alternative is to use mental commands to achieve the same goal. Progressive relaxation is one of the most effective techniques for relieving body tension.

PROGRESSIVE RELAXATION

Sit or lie comfortably. Focus your attention on your feet. Push down with the heels, and spread and flex your toes. Hold, hold, hold the tension…then release. Now curl the toes under, raise the heels like a ballerina, press, press, press…and release. Next, push down with the heels, spread the toes and wiggle your feet and ankles from side to side, up and down. Relax the feet. Feel fatigue leave your feet.

Now focus your awareness on your legs. Contract the calf and thigh muscles. And hold, hold, hold the tension…then release. Once again, contract the calf and thigh muscles. And hold, hold, hold…and release. Your legs are heavy; feel their heaviness. Next, focus on your hips, buttocks and stomach muscles. Inhale comfortably. Squeeze the buttock muscles. Squeeze and tense the muscles. Pull in the belly button. Squeeze and hold, then, exhale, release…relax…let go…melt…like liquid butter.

> Let your arms fall softly to your side. Make a tight fist. Tense the arms, the biceps, the triceps. Hold, hold, hold the tension…and release. Feel…experience your arms hollow. Arms hang loosely, palms down, fingers toward the earth. Let the worries of the day drain out of long arms into the earth. Spread your fingers wide, curl and open. Stretch the fingers…then relax them. Relax, release, and feel the sensation inside the hand. Hands like an empty glove.
>
> Now gently roll your head from side to side…start with your ear against the left shoulder. Slowly roll your head to the right shoulder. With your right hand gently rub the long line from hairline to shoulder blade and back…to release that tension. When you reach the shoulder again, make a fist and lightly rub the shoulder area. Gently tap the shoulder and neck while rolling the shoulder forward and backward. That feels good. Now do the same for the other side. Now focus on your face. Raise your eyebrows, press your tongue to the roof of your mouth. Hold the tension… then release. Next, massage around the eyebrows and cheekbones. Gently stroke your eyelids and eyelashes. Massage your forehead, temples, jaw and chin.
>
> Enjoy the tingle and warmth as tension dissolves throughout your body. Languish in this serenity. Then, when you are ready, slowly open your eyes. May you carry this peaceful serenity with you throughout the night. Namaste. Progressive Relaxation.

When you step out of the tub, have a warm towel, slippers and a robe waiting. *Sweet dreams…*

At first, **Dawn**, the stressed single parent, didn't think she could manage all the logistics of taking a whole day away from her full plate of responsibilities. But her eyes were opened when she realized she could enjoy a nightly **spa experience at home**. The first time around she organized her evening so that every chore was done and the children in bed by 9:00 PM. She turned off the phones, arranged her special bath with spa paraphernalia she'd purchased and played dreamy music throughout.

Dawn relaxed completely for the first time in a long while. According to her, she couldn't remember ever feeling so peaceful. She vowed then and there to give herself this small luxury once a week. Dawn continues to seek opportunities to nurture and reward herself in little ways on a daily basis.

Nicole, the successful career woman, began practicing several of the relaxation techniques and exercises in *When You Need a Timeout* to "quiet her nerves," as she put it. She practiced **self-hypnosis for relaxation** to ease the knots in her stomach whenever thoughts of her illness became obsessive. She joined an evening stretch-and-tone class at the local Y to help her unwind. Eventually she was able to **reframe** how she would handle an unfavorable medical diagnosis.

Nicole learned to put herself in a calm, relaxed state by practicing **progressive relaxation** and **calming breath** exercises before bedtime. She also began drinking a cup of chamomile tea each night before retiring. This routine helped ease her into a more restful state. It didn't take long before Nicole was enjoying a sound night's sleep. Goodbye, insomnia.

PART THREE

Creative Escapes:
The Art of Relaxation

Chapter Ten

Living the Life You Love

*G*OOD morning...good morning! Your **Getaway Day** is finally here. You're ready to pursue the activities you love. This is *your* day, and you'll want to enjoy every moment of it. Plan to rise early—6:00 or 7:00 AM. You won't want to miss one minute of your day of indulgence! Open your heart to all you anticipate this wonderful day to be.

BE IN THE MOMENT

This is going to be an upbeat day; no recriminations, no reliving bad memories, no problems to resolve. You've already worked through all of that. Instead, you will be living in the moment, taking time to appreciate and enjoy the world around you. Getting to do the things you love. That's the tone to set for today.

You may be nervous about following through on some goals today. That's normal. Reframe that to "I am excited about following through on my goal today!" Get up and greet the day with self-affirming talk. Choose affirmations that have meaning to you. Think them, say them, and see how they improve your outlook. Consider the following:

> ## *Positive Thoughts*
>
> Your thoughts set the tone for the day. If you could choose your thoughts, wouldn't they be self-affirming and confidence building? That's what affirmations are: positive thoughts about yourself to yourself. Make them part of your morning routine and watch your attitude and self-esteem soar.
>
> As you head for the shower each morning, begin to ask yourself questions or think positive thoughts designed to start your day with good feelings. Questions such as "If I count my blessings, what would I find that is good in my life?" "What am I grateful for?" "Who am I grateful for?"
>
> Allow yourself to feel the emotions these questions evoke. Be in the moment. Positive thoughts such as "I'm a good person and I deserve to be happy"; "I love myself just as I am"; "I am calm, relaxed and confident and can handle all my challenges today"; or "I am truly blessed" empower you. Choose questions and affirmations that are meaningful to you. Write them down and post them where they can easily be seen first thing in the morning.
>
> Breathe slowly, inhaling positive energy and light deep down into your soul. Hold your breath. Exhale and reflect. You have chosen to focus on the good in your life this morning. What you think about determines how you feel. How do you feel now? What is your mood now? Positive Thoughts.

When **Cassidy**, the career-oriented newlywed, began practicing the **Positive Thoughts** exercise, her thoughts always drifted to the state of her marriage. So many negative thoughts and feelings. She hated that every time she and her spouse had this discussion about children versus her career, it deteriorated into a shouting match. It was an understatement to say that things were tense at home. No more laughter...

The fact is, the dynamics of love can be very stressful. This powerful force can make us feel happy, sad, insecure, confident, angry or in perfect harmony with our partner. Cassidy dared risk the question she was trying to avoid: Had she fallen out of love with her husband? An honest examination was pivotal to their future as husband and wife.

Cassidy found her thoughts going back to the things she loved about her marriage and the qualities that drew her to her husband in the first place. **Positive thoughts.** His sensitivity was one of his charming and endearing qualities. She wondered why she felt she could not talk to him about her need to develop and grow in her field and postpone, at least temporarily, having their baby.

Cassidy set up a romantic dinner date for the two of them—just the right atmosphere to have this kind of heart-to-heart. The only ground rule was to let each other talk without interruption. Many misconceptions were aired and cleared up that night. They talked about their hopes and dreams for the future and began to reconnect. Both needed to **reframe** their priorities along the way and put themselves in the other's shoes. Their open and honest conversation ended with a vow not to let their different points of view get so out of hand again. In the end both she and her hubby found a happy compromise. And yes, future plans include career and baby.

HAVE A GREAT DAY FROM MORNING TILL NIGHT!

Grab your bag, tickets, schedules and whatever else completes your adventure. Spend the day doing what you enjoy, indulging... those activities that bring pleasure and make you smile. Have the time of your life...a great day from morning till night!

Maybe your idea is to have an enjoyable day to reflect and rejuvenate yourself. The simple pleasures will make you happy. All you want is to climb into a tub full of scented bubbles, have breakfast in bed, eating from your best china, buy two dozen roses just for you, get a massage, manicure and pedicure, spend all day at a day spa, find time to read a good book, laugh or cry watching a video or a matinee. In other words, if your dream for a getaway is a day of self-nurturing, following are three "feel-good" scenarios for you.

SCENARIO 1:
Kicking Back With a Good Book

Start the day with a morning stroll. Select a safe and tranquil destination, but don't plan your route. Let your feet take you where they want to go. Enjoy the novelty of wandering without forethought. Be open to new experiences. See the world with soft eyes. Notice the sights, sounds and colors that surround you. Feel the wind on your cheek, the sun on your face. Observe nature all around you. Take a deep breath and smell the fresh morning air.

Think about the interactions you have had in the past that renewed your faith in people. Simple acts of kindness. Vow to project that feeling towards others, unconditionally, today. Give away a smile to everyone you meet. Greet a stranger. Say "Good morning," "Hello," "Please," "Excuse me" or "Thank you" to someone. Allow someone ahead of you in a line, assist someone in need—you get the picture. Helping others is an enriching experience. You'll receive instant gratification from their acknowledgment, and you'll have made someone's day a little brighter.

When you return home, prepare a breakfast that excites all your senses. Set the table with your favorite flowers. Use your fancy crystal and china. You're worth it! Surround yourself with the things you love. Use your imagination to create serene spaces—your theme for the day. You've booked a massage therapist for an at-home massage. Hmmm, heaven! Then spend the rest of your day lounging, or on your favorite hobby or kicking back with a good book. Whatever you have planned, relax and enjoy your dream day!

SCENARIO 2: *Day Spa-ing*

If your desire is for an athletic start to the day, allow ten or fifteen minutes to warm up before undertaking any activity, including walking. Focus on movements that emphasize body awareness. As a result you'll not only achieve a higher level of comfort, but you'll enjoy the exercise more. You'll be tuned in to your body's feedback and can adjust your movements accordingly. Yoga stretches, side rolls and standing body circles are examples of warm-up routines that fit this category. Stretch the quads and calves. These exercises not only increase flexibility but help dissipate mental and physical tension. They help you feel relaxed long after completing the exercises.

After some simple morning stretches to increase flexibility and get the blood circulating, you are ready to get out and enjoy the morning air. Take your MP3 player and listen to your favorite music while enjoying a brisk walk, jog or bike ride. Or better yet, leave your music at home and instead listen to the sound of

When You Need A Timeout

Cassidy's research led her to a space camp experience for an astronaut adventure of her own. The simulated rides created sensations similar to those of flying a spaceship, blasting up from a virtual runway to a make-believe stratosphere. She was on a space shuttle mission; she was directing the lunar rover mission. She was a space traveler watching a simulated sky and stars and a 360-degree glimpse of Earth; experiencing what three times the force of gravity on Earth feels like; handling spatial disorientation and oxygen deprivation at 100,000 feet; and learning to punch out of a cockpit from an ejection seat. At the end of a most satisfying getaway, Cassidy observed that she had "boldly gone where no man has gone before" (the *Star Trek* opening monologue—as every "Trekkie" knows!).

Toni, the widow, gathered her courage and took a bold step for her getaway adventure. She would do something she had been considering for months—every time she looked into the mirror. The past year of wallowing in her misery had taken a toll on her physical appearance. She looked old, not at all like her former self. Her complexion was dull, her cheeks were sunken, and she had deep folds around her nose and mouth. The only thing missing was the "turkey neck" sag, for which she was grateful. She decided to get some cosmetic work done—to do something special just for her.

This decision did not come easily, considering her finances. But after some soul searching she decided to take a small portion of the Hawaii money and put it to good use—helping her feel better about herself now. She had already adjusted to the fact that retirement was not in her near future, and she knew she would be diligent about replacing her savings.

Toni was sure she did not want cosmetic surgery. She was

looking into procedures promising minimally invasive facial rejuvenation. After several consultations with licensed cosmetic surgeons, she found the package for her. In a relaxed, spa-like facility Toni had a complete facial that included a micro-dermabrasion peel and collagen injections to fill out her nasolabial folds and cheeks. The results were immediate. Her skin was smoother, firmer and brighter. The lines around her nose and mouth were softened. And most important, everything looked natural. An update to her hairdo and a manicure and pedicure completed her transformation.

The change in how she looked and felt was priceless to Toni. Now every time she looks in the mirror she finds herself humming the lyrics, "Don't cha wish your girlfriend was hot like me…," from the Pussycat Dolls song; and this makes her *laugh out loud*. She feels good inside and outside now. The perky, energetic (and now vivacious) Toni is back!

Chapter Eleven

If You Want My Body......

Spa services are often extensive and can be overwhelming to the beginner. Most spas offer head-to-toe selections including facial, dermabrasion, manicure, aromatherapy, body wrap, hydrotherapy, bikini wax, reflexology and pedicure, to name just a few services on the menu. However, the number one body treatment associated with spas, by far, is the body massage. And there is a massage to fit every need:

SOOTHING SPA TREATMENTS

- **Swedish Massage**—Long, light, soothing strokes designed to improve circulation, skin and muscle tone and create an overall sense of harmony.
- **Aromatherapy Massage**—Swedish massage using essential oils to relax and detoxify the body while promoting a tranquil mood.
- **Deep Tissue Massage**—Deep, firm pressure strokes designed to relieve muscle tension, pain and toxic buildup and ease tired joints.
- **Hot Stone Massage**—Combines Swedish massage with

smooth, heated stones placed on key meridian points on the body; warming the muscles, joints and creating a deep state of relaxation. The warmed stones are gently run across the body in a rhythmic flowing massage to melt away stress and tension.
- **Sports Massage**—Relieves stiffness from sports-related injuries or arthritis. Reduces muscle tension and pain.
- **Stress Buster Massage**—Mini massage for the head, neck, back and shoulders. May combine Swedish and deep tissue techniques. Relieves tension, soothes tired muscles.
- **Prenatal Massage**—Specially designed to alleviate the aches and pains of expectant mothers using safe, effective techniques for comfort and total relaxation.
- **Reflexology**—Soothing stimulation of foot pressure points using acupressure and massage to reestablish energy flow throughout the body, relieve stress and promote relaxation.

No matter which body treatment you select, you'll enjoy a relaxing vacation from the stressed emotions and weary spirit with which you arrived. You'll find that taking time to pamper yourself will result in feeling better about yourself. And few things boost your self-confidence more than feeling better about yourself.

Julia, of the "sandwich generation", opted for an overnight spa retreat getaway and reported she had a wonderful day. "Twenty-four hours away from my everyday stress exposed me to a whole new way of being. I realized that I deserve to treat myself to a day away periodically. It's a must for anyone dealing with as much day-to-day stress as I have. I came home feeling refreshed, renewed and so completely relaxed that no one, not even my family, can push me that close to the edge again. I now know that I can take measures to fortify myself for facing the tensions of my everyday life.

"Sometime during my day of leisure and spa pampering I gained clarity on some pressing problems. I developed an action plan, if you will, on ways to communicate more assertively and effectively with my parents and son. I am thankful for everything I learned about myself from doing the self-help exercises; about taking time away from stress, and about making myself a priority. I now have the courage to express how I think, feel and believe in a more direct, open and honest way."

Dawn, the single parent, was given a spa gift certificate for her birthday. She had never been to a spa before and was a little nervous about what to expect. In addition, she had a few "delicate" questions she needed answered before her appointment.

Q. First of all, do I have to remove all my clothes for the massage?

> **A.** Not if you don't feel comfortable about it. Although you will have to remove your bra for the back and shoulder massage, panties are optional. Most spas supply a robe and slippers to change into. The massage therapist waits outside the room while you disrobe and slip under the sheet on the massage table. Draped towels discreetly protect your privacy at all times.

Q. What part of my body do they massage? What's off limits?

A. Depending on the massage therapist, every limb and muscle mass from the top of your head to your toes, excluding the breasts and buttocks, will be worked on—although there are some massage therapists who are very thorough and include the muscles of the buttocks. If this or any part of the massage is uncomfortable to you, just tell the therapist. They make every effort to relax you and put you at ease. In fact, the first question they'll ask is if you've ever had a massage before. Your answer is their cue to be open to explanations about each step of the process.

Q. I really don't think I'd be comfortable having a man massage me. Do I have any options?

A. Yes. When you make the appointment, request a woman massage therapist. You'll find, though, that there are women who prefer a male. These women usually like deep, sports massages and feel a man can apply more pressure. In my experience, the smallest woman you can imagine gave me the deepest, most satisfying massage. (Although when she hopped up on the table with me and started contorting my calves and legs into pretzels, I was ready to holler uncle!)

Q. What can I expect when I arrive for my appointment? What is expected of me?

A. You should arrive at least a half hour early. At the reception desk, an attendant will give you a key and show you to the ladies' locker room. You can ask for a tour and get instructions on how to use the facilities at this time. You'll change into the robe and slippers that are provided. If anything is missing, let the attendant or someone at the desk know. Take a nice, hot shower to begin relaxing your body. Then try the sauna, steam room and Jacuzzi to relax further. The spa atmosphere and soft music will further enhance your experience of calming relaxation. Enjoy the spa amenities of fresh fruit, teas, juices and water in the waiting area. Your therapist will come for you at your appointment time. Then there's nothing left to do but enjoy your spa experience!

"I never knew anything could feel so good and I could feel so rested," **Dawn** reported after her first spa experience. "Ever since that day, my family knows not to even ask what I want for my birthday. They know all I want is to spend my birthday relaxing at a spa. Spending a day being pampered for a change is such a treat. I come back home feeling so refreshed that it takes a day or two for me to get worked up to my usual level of stress!"

Chapter Twelve

Let's Get Physical

Spending a day at the spa getting pampered and relaxing was once thought to be a self-indulgent pastime mostly for the rich. That perception has changed. The health benefits alone have made many of these services worth the "splurge" for the average person. In fact, some health plans will reimburse you for targeted alternative treatments, particularly when prescribed by a physician.

East and West are beginning to meet when it comes to the medical establishment. This is due mostly to the fact that the number of people seeking gentler alternatives and choosing to take preventive measures for optimal health is growing. Needless to say, the known risks and side effects of some prescription drugs play a big part in this growing trend. Conversely, the benefits of using relaxation and stress management techniques for improving one's physical and mental health are becoming more mainstream, thanks in part to studies funded by the National Institutes of Health's National Center for Complementary and Alternative Medicine.

Today it's not hard to find teaching hospitals and other medical facilities that offer complementary and alternative medicine

(CAM) or integrative medicine in conjunction with cancer treatment, pre- and post-surgery, childbirth preparation, treatment of irritable bowel syndrome and chronic pain as well as for calming fears of patients who need dental procedures. Besides relief from pain, some benefits of alternative therapies include speedier healing of injuries, shorter hospital stays and swifter convalescence. Anecdotal evidence includes patients' experiencing greater physical, mental, emotional and spiritual well-being.

While there are skeptics and critics in the medical profession who doubt the efficacy of some alternative procedures, there is ample evidence that psychological stress compromises the immune system. There are a multitude of studies that look at the effects of stress on people's health, and few dispute the benefits that deep relaxation and stress-reduction protocols have on patient wellness. Besides massage, you might find mainstream hospitals offering Reiki, acupuncture, hypnosis and reflexology as part of your treatment modality:

Popular Alternative Therapies

- **Reiki**—Or energy therapy (sometimes called "healing touch"), is an ancient Japanese healing tradition for stress reduction and relaxation that also promotes healing. The essence of Reiki is to unblock and rebalance the body via hand placement over key energy points or Chakras.
- **Acupuncture**—An ancient Chinese energy therapy using fine needles inserted at meridian points to unblock the body's energy flow or "chi" to relax "locked" muscles, unblock sinuses and relieve pain. Chi is believed to be the fundamental force of health and well-being in traditional Chinese medicine.
- **Hypnosis**—Approved by the American Medical Association over fifty years ago for use in medicine, hypnosis uses introspection through dialogue with the

subconscious (trance), concentration to focus on the presented problem and deep relaxation to foster physical and emotional healing by uncovering the body's innate ability for self-healing.
- **Reflexology**—A massage technique to reestablish energy flow throughout the body by stimulating reflex points on the bottom of the feet and/or hands. Relieves stress and promotes deep relaxation in specific body parts linked to those reflex points.

Toni has been diagnosed with osteopenia. She wanted to avoid at all cost coming down with the debilitating, bone-thinning disease of osteoporosis. In addition, because of some reported risks of side effects, Toni could not see herself taking prescription drugs for the rest of her life. She asked her doctor for alternatives and was relieved when he recommended she begin doing weight-bearing exercises to slow the rate of bone loss. Toni found out that exercises like running, brisk walking, gardening, stair climbing, dancing and tennis all fit the bill. These activities make the body work against gravity, and the physical impact stimulates bone formation. Toni's doctor recommended she start out slowly with the gentler weight-bearing exercises such as walking, since she had not exercised in a long time.

Toni joined a gym for women and started out on the treadmill, then graduated to low-impact aerobics. She observed that many of the women her age and older also took weight-resistance (weight-lifting) classes, and she had a fruitful conversation with one woman who had been diagnosed with osteoporosis three years earlier. Because the prescription medicine for her condition caused stomach problems, the woman began weight-lifting and weight-bearing exercises. Her most recent bone scan, she confided, showed that she had *increased* bone density compared with her earlier reading. Toni was astounded to learn that that this agile lady was almost eighty years old! You guessed it...the very next time it was offered, Toni joined the weight-resistance class.

PART FOUR

What a Difference a Day Makes

Chapter Thirteen

It's Time to Call It a Day

At the end of the day, take a quiet evening stroll. This is your time for meditative thought. Replay the events of your day in your mind. You've just spent an entire day listening to your own heart...enjoying your own pleasurable pursuits—your ideal day. You conscientiously set aside worries, problems and the search for solutions. During quiet times you were alone with your thoughts, listening to your own body.

What truths have you learned about yourself, about the world around you? Was it that doing things you genuinely enjoy opens your heart toward others—especially your loved ones? That showing compassion and caring towards others comes back to you multiplied? That the world is not so bad and there are some pretty nice people in it? And did you find that you are stronger and more resilient than you thought—able to go with the flow and take some risks? Perhaps you learned not to take yourself so seriously. That laughter relieves your stress. That letting go of anger and guilt towards yourself and others is a freeing experience. Or maybe you were surprised that the answer to your most perplexing problem was right in front of you all the time.

Meditate:

Experience the power of **meditation.** Set aside five or ten minutes of quiet, peaceful time with yourself. Gradually work up to twenty minutes several times a week. The benefits of continual practice include lower blood pressure and pulse rate, lower stress hormones in the blood, reduced wear and tear on the body and mind and a raised pain threshold.

At times when you want to reflect deeply on a specific subject or solve a problem or make a decision under stress, try meditating. If you're looking for it, inspiration will find you during these quiet times. The following is an easy **meditation** technique to practice:

1. Focus on one thought at a time.
2. Pose your question or dilemma.
3. State the outcome you need. Be precise at this point.
4. Stay focused on your contemplation. Let go of other thoughts that may intrude (and they will). Adopt a passive attitude. Do not judge or critique them. Let them pass like soft clouds drifting across the sky. Then deliberately turn your attention back to your question.
5. Don't try to force an answer. It may not come at this time. But like an elusive name or word that suddenly pops into your mind, your answer *will* come. You'll know it because you'll feel good about it. You'll have an "I've got it!" moment.

Any empowering thoughts about what you want to do, what you want your future to be? Does your life reflect your true dreams? Or have you settled for a lot less? Expect some insights, maybe an epiphany, during your meditations.

It's Time to Call It a Day

Nicole had such an epiphany. It hit during her weekend getaway adventure. Nicole's vision of an ideal day was to work with her hands, volunteering for a program like Habitat for Humanity. So off she flew to New Orleans to assist in the cleanup efforts after Hurricane Katrina. The sense of pride and satisfaction she felt helping others that day gave her pause. "To my family I was always the 'success story,' always independent, the pride of the family," she acknowledged. "As a result I set high standards of independence for myself. After all, didn't everyone expect that of me?"

But her day away showed her that accepting help from others in no way diminishes the recipient. And in fact, the person giving assistance gets a great deal of inner satisfaction, a feeling of contributing in a time of crisis when helping someone in need. Nicole continued, "I decided then and there to confide in my family and close friends about my health challenges and need for their assistance. Everyone rallied around me and was more than happy to help out. Reconnecting in this way, on a personal level, was just beautiful! And, in fact, my family and I are closer now than ever. I'm so grateful. The outpouring of love from family and friends is very humbling. For the first time in my life I feel I can finally let my guard down…and exhale."

Chapter Fourteen

Self-Discovery— There's Joy in Being Me

Write down your thoughts and feelings about all you experienced today. Include the places, people and emotions you encountered. Describe the colors, sounds and smells that swirled around you. Make it vivid; capture that *joie de vivre*!

Journaling:

If you don't keep one, think about starting a **journal** now. It can be a useful tool in your stress-management arsenal. Journaling provides an outlet for your private feelings and emotions, a place where you can express yourself as openly as you like. Journal notes can be cathartic, healing, problem solving and a boost to your self-esteem. Allow your thoughts to flow from pen to paper for fifteen or twenty minutes a day. Don't edit or worry about grammar. The only rule is to be true to yourself. This journal can serve as future reference, chronicling where you've been and where you're going from this day forward.

When You Need A Timeout

When Dawn began **journaling**, she found it helped release a lot of pent-up stress. She unburdened the challenges of her day and got out a lot of anger while writing. She enjoyed the feeling of empowerment it gave her to say what was really on her mind. She furiously wrote the words she dared not say to her boss, for example, since she needed to keep her job. She lamented how hard her life was raising two children alone; how hard it was living from paycheck to paycheck. All of the emotions she successfully pushed below the surface every day were released in her writing. And it felt good! Nightly journaling eventually replaced the fattening foods Dawn used to turn to when she needed to relieve her anxiety and frustrations.

As *you* write, think about those burdens you left behind for a day. Perhaps you've decided you don't need them anymore. Just leave them. Maybe you've learned that the past no longer has power over you. That you choose to live in the present and that you can counter negative self-talk with positive affirmations. You won't sweat the small stuff! You've learned that you are in control of your world and that the choice to feel good about yourself is yours. And you choose to focus on the good times and self-affirming memories. Perhaps your epiphany was that when you feel good, the world treats you better. Pleasing body, mind and spirit is now a permanent part of your schedule. Isn't that grrrreat!

Toni had read somewhere that depression was really anger turned inward. She found a grain of truth in that statement when she began **journaling** her thoughts. Up to that time Toni had blamed her employer for her paltry pension. After all, they were the ones who administered the pension plan. She depended on them to make profitable investments, and they should have been looking out for her welfare. After all, didn't they owe that much to loyal long-time, "the company comes first" employees like Toni?

By expressing her thoughts in writing, Toni was able to come to terms with the fact that she was ultimately the one responsible for her present circumstances. Toni was angry at herself! First of all, she should have paid attention to her retirement fund years earlier. Not waited until three months before retirement to find out the state of her affairs. She could have armed herself with the knowledge necessary to watch her investments. She could have sought advice from her coworkers who had kept their eyes on their retirement funds and fared better than she did. They moved their money into safer, less aggressive funds as they got closer to retirement. All employees had that option.

Toni's new perspective was just what she needed to move forward and get on with her life. The choice was always hers.

LIFE IS WHAT YOU MAKE IT

Maybe during your getaway you've vowed that no matter how busy you are, you will do one thing each day that brings you joy. Maybe you found that when you feel good it's easy to bestow love on those around you. Or just maybe you've discovered a new path that gives meaning to your life. Maybe you finally found what you were put on this earth to do. And to paraphrase Dr. Benjamin E. Mays, "Every man and woman is born into the world to do something unique and distinctive…and if *you* don't do it, it will never be done." Now that's profound!

Jennifer rediscovered her artistic talent as a result of the **visualization** and **journaling** exercises. "I always loved drawing and painting growing up. I had talent, according to my teachers. As a teenager, I entered art contests and displayed work in local talent shows. I even entertained dreams of becoming a fashion illustrator. But once I married and had children, I never seemed to have time to pursue it. The fact is, once I became involved in an art project, it became almost all-consuming. Time flew when I painted. And I'd get caught up in the zeal of creativity, to the detriment of other responsibilities. Unfortunately, there was only room in my life for one all-consuming love at a time. Between the two there was no contest—my family won hands down.

"But now I have the time. I enrolled in a series of art workshops on the day of my getaway. I spent my day away sketching and painting in an artist's studio. I felt so alive! That was truly an ideal day—pursuing my passion! I'm spending my days now in creative escape…with a paint brush—not a wine glass—in my hand."

SELF-DISCOVERY—THERE'S JOY IN BEING ME

My Day Away Journal

When You Need A Timeout

Chapter Fifteen

There's Always Something

*I*F you haven't already guessed it, the hidden lesson in *When You Need a Timeout* is, don't wait until everything is "just right" before you do some of the things you want to do. Because, as you know from past experience, there will always be something that comes up and demands your attention. Life needs balance. Putting out fires shouldn't be the sum total of your life. Use some of that energy doing what you love instead. From now on, when you find yourself in pain physically, emotionally or spiritually, understand that it's alright to say *When You Need a Timeout*—and take it!

I'VE GOT A NEW ATTITUDE

Cassidy learned that she had to be proactive and take steps to balance the demands of marriage and pursuing a career. "Remembering what attracted me to my husband in the first place put my marriage/career quandary into perspective. The loving feelings those memories brought back—well, that love was a treasure I did not want to lose. Communicating those feelings and being open to compromise—that was the key for me. To think the breakdown in communication almost cost us our marriage!

"Sure, I'm going to pursue my career. Now, while there's still just the two of us. It's the optimal time. And yes, when weighing the demands of marriage versus career, sometimes one may have to take precedence. But for sure, I don't intend to let pursuing a career interfere with the closeness of my relationship with my husband again. It's not always about work, you know. And that's the delicate balance all working women have to find a way to achieve.

"The self-help and stress-reduction techniques I learned leading up to my day away from everyday stress, all helped me redefine what was most important to me—my marriage. And best of all, they helped me realize that I have choices. I can be flexible. I can enjoy separate interests while still making my marriage a high priority. The balance that I needed—and my vow—is to always make time for the romance in my life even while pursuing compelling outside interests."

Dawn, overworked and underappreciated, began to take a good look at her life. "The children are a handful right now, with their high energy and demands. Although, I have to admit, some of the things they do and say simply fascinate me. They're so cute and come up with some of the most insightful observations. How did these clever little people come from me? When I can take a breath, I feel blessed because of them. And thanks to practicing the relaxation techniques I know how to find my space, my solitude when I just want to be. I know there is light at the end of the tunnel. My children are growing up fast. And the older they get, the more I am able to depend on them to help out at home.

"My job is another story. My boss is a very negative person but I always felt with my situation I had to resign myself to taking what he dishes out. After all, I have to work and take care of my two children! But you know what…I don't have to work here. My day away gave me time to realize that I needed to take responsibility and put myself first. As the children grow, my priorities will change. I need to plan now what I want out of life. What steps can I take right now, today, to position myself for better job opportunities?

"I decided to go to Human Resources to find a new job within my company. I found out that my company will pay education expenses for employees who want to upgrade their job qualifications. I had a confidential discussion with the personnel director about my options and how to qualify for this benefit package. In a nutshell, I've decided to enroll in a college that evaluates my job skills and prior education to apply towards a degree program.

"I'm nervous and excited about this new road I'm taking. Thanks to all the self-help exercises and the 'getaway from stress' day, I've had time to think about my future. Something I've never had time to think about before. I have more confidence in myself these days. I'm taking it slow, as this adds another layer of responsibility to my busy life. But did I mention how excited I am? For the first time in a long time I believe there's hope—even for me."

Jennifer had a life that most women would envy. She had a beautiful home, well-behaved children and a husband who was a good provider. "So why was I in such a self-destructive mode? The stress reduction techniques and 'time for me' getaway day allowed me to reflect on who I was and what I wanted out of life. I realized I hadn't developed much of a life beyond the needs of my family.

"So, if I wasn't happy with my appearance, for example, what was I going to do about it? I'd tried and rejected the health-club route before because I really didn't like to exercise. But I did like to dance—back in the day—and one of the offerings at the gym was belly dancing. I joined. I enjoy the classes tremendously and especially look forward to the camaraderie with the other women.

Not only am I having fun, I'm beginning to feel sexier—a side benefit of the class!

"Since money was never a problem, I've decided to ease my way back into the workforce by working through a temporary agency. This way I can hone some rusty skills and keep abreast of trends in the workforce. Eventually I will take the steps necessary for full-time employment. For now it feels good to have the extra income to spend any way I choose. Being the consummate mom, I spend a lot on extras for the kids. But I also spend money on me. Besides my art courses, I need my 'beauty fixes.' You know, makeup, hair, nails and occasional spa treatments. The added bonus—my husband's interest and romantic attention is once again where it should be—on me!"

Nicole, strong-willed, independent, empowered, could not believe the sense of relief she felt letting others see her vulnerable. "My reality check didn't come about in just one 'getaway,' but gradually. Going through and experiencing all of the self-help and relaxation exercises and self-help techniques helped me heal spiritually. I needed to find forgiveness, compassion and even humor in my heart once again. And I needed to let others into my life. That may seem simple for others, but believe me, it was no small task for me.

"I also realized that the specter of my illness had defined me for the better part of the year. From the time I felt the lump, I had become the illness. The more I tried to ignore it, the bigger the 'C' word loomed. And the more I tried to ignore it. Fear kept me stuck in a vicious loop I couldn't get out of. Where were those attributes that helped to make me a success in my career? Where was fearless Nicole?

"That's where I am now—finding me again. First of all, I've gotten my finances in order. I was in better shape than I thought. Thanks to many of the exercises that seemed to speak to me personally, I realized that all work and no personal life is a life out of balance. It's no longer the lifestyle I want. I now know that showing vulnerability to those I care about is not a sign of weakness on my part. I enjoy the love and support—of knowing I have family and friends I can depend on. People with whom I can share my journey…and share the love in me. This soul searching also gave me the strength to face my cancer fear. I finally went to the doctor to get that biopsy. I was on pins and needles waiting for the results. The good news, the growth was benign. I felt like I'd gotten my life back!

"Anti-climactic maybe. After all there was no adverse health issue to worry about. Had I gone to the doctor when I first felt the lump I could have saved myself months of anguish and sleepless nights. But I know now that sometimes things happen for a reason. There was a lesson to be learned from all of my drama. For me, it was a need for change in the way I lived. For all my stoic independence, deep down I needed to feel protected too. I needed to be able to let go sometime, to exhale, if you will. My self-imposed independence was a lonely existence. Helping others in their time of need and asking help in my time of need was one of the most enriching experiences of my life. I can't argue with the results. I feel like I got a second chance—and this may sound corny—but a second chance to live my life!"

Julia is reaping the benefits of managing her stress by practicing daily relaxation routines. "I've become so motivated that I've started to exercise and eat healthier. I find I have more energy these days. Another benefit is that I found the calm I needed to reach constructive decisions. This is where I needed to be before I could deal with my issues with my son.

"He is the love of my life and always will be. Since his father and I separated when my son was a toddler, it's always been the just two of us. I blamed my husband for leaving us and for everything at first. But to be honest, he asked me to leave with him, and I wouldn't go. It's a long story, but we lived with my parents at the time. My mother convinced me it would be best for me and her grandchild to stay—in a stable environment with them—until my husband proved he was 'a man' and could take care of a family. As always, I bowed to my mother's will. But that's ancient history now. Thanks to the stress-reduction techniques and exercises I've begun to come to terms with my past.

"There's nothing I wouldn't do for my son. And now I realize that that's a big part of the problem. I'm a big part of the problem. I still treat this adult as if he was still a child. When he came back home—just until he could get himself together, as he said—I fell right back into the mommy routine. I washed his clothes, cleaned his room, made his meals and gave him money when he asked. Of course, I expected him to observe my curfew, call me when he expected to be late, get up early to look for a job and so on. I even set the alarm on his clock to be sure he got up on time!

"I've slowly come to realize that I've already raised this child. There's nothing more I can do. If I want my son to behave as an adult, I have to treat him as an adult. So some big changes have been going on around our house. We've had long heart-to-heart talks where I listen more and offer advice less. We both agreed on the need for concrete plans for his future, and I'm proud to say, my son has imposed some stringent deadlines on himself for meeting those goals. The other day he confessed to me that he was not at all happy to be still 'living off Mom' at his age. But he needed this wake-up call to be able to move on. I've seen the changes in him. He's taking more responsibility, thinking of my needs and assuming a more mature role in our relationship. I'm proud of my son and I'm confident he's headed in the right direction now.

"My life is so much more pleasant these days. I'm happier. Sometimes even exuberant. Yes, there are still a lot of stressors and a lot I still have to work through. But I practice stress-management and relaxation techniques every day. I'm happy to say that as a result a lot of that stress is the positive kind—the Good Stress."

Toni started reminiscing about her life prior to this last year. "My husband died ten years ago and left me a small insurance policy. There was no pension plan where he worked. After I paid up our bills, I used what was left as a down payment on my townhouse. I could swing the mortgage on my salary alone, with money left over. Some of that extra money was designated for the travel club my girlfriends and I started several years ago. Every couple of years we vacationed at some sunny resort with the money we pooled together. I have so many good memories from those trips. They gave me a lot to look forward to.

"If I could give one piece of advice at my age it would be this: 'To every young person out there, you are never too young to plan your retirement. Be informed about all aspects of your life that involve your welfare. Don't leave it up to anyone else!'

"With that said, this last year has been a trial and a triumph for me. I guess you're never too old to learn a life lesson, and I've added another to my store of experiences. The self-help exercises I learned were invaluable to me. I've made some short- and long-range plans to ensure a comfortable retirement. I've already begun to save a larger portion of my paycheck in anticipation of retirement. I'll have to wait two more years longer until I'm eligible for full social security. That money, added to my pension, will enable me to handle my debt obligations without having to scrape by.

"The best thing to come from all this is my growing confidence in myself. Although it sounds like an oxymoron, but indulging myself—in positive ways, not emotional this time—was the best thing I could do for myself. When I thought I had nowhere else to go, the self-help exercises and stress-management techniques helped me see my troubles had new solutions. The change began within me, grew my confidence and then allowed me to be comfortable with making physical improvements on the outside. Some would call that vain, but I knew deep inside that I needed all of the above to turn around that feeling of being useless, stupid and old.

"I'm more active, both physically and mentally, than I was a year ago. I'm looking forward to a retirement full of the joy of living. I intend to live the rest of my life with this outlook—live, love, laugh until you die. When life gave me lemons, I'm happy to say I learned to make the sweetest lemonade!

"Oh yes, our Hawaiian vacation will be postponed for a few years more…but my friends insist we save that trip for my new retirement date. My eyes are wide open this time. This vacation/retirement celebration will happen as planned."

Chapter Sixteen

Live Your Life

When we started this journey, I asked you to make a promise to yourself—to spend an entire day on you, doing wonderful things for you, just you and only you. In return I offered to show you how to live that day free of worries and responsibilities. To get a day away without feeling guilty, while doing only those things that brought you joy and pleasure. So, did you take my offer?

If you did, if you followed the road laid out for you, you no doubt realized that *When You Need a Timeout* wasn't about the destination. The journey was the ultimate goal. The journey gave you time for introspection, to listen to your inner voice and connect with your natural wisdom. Along the way you learned how to handle stress by changing destructive self-talk to positive affirmations. You learned how to change a bad situation by reframing its meaning. You learned relaxation, visualization and meditation for clarity, problem solving and "eureka"—a new understanding of an old worry.

You learned what it means to be good to yourself, to nurture the inner you with self-pampering and quiet walks. You learned to visualize beautiful moments from your store of wonderful memories and some relaxation techniques to help re-create the mood.

You learned how to play again, to reawaken dreams, to live out a fantasy and to greet each day drinking in the beauty of nature.

And perhaps best of all, you learned to forgive—yourself and others; to repair strained relations and to change fundamental beliefs about what you are entitled to. You learned what it means to live in the moment and reconnect with the important people and things in your life.

A New Way of Being

Maybe your shift was subtle, not profound. But notice a change in your way of relating from now on—your way of being. When you have to, you're not afraid to ask the hard questions, because you now have the skills to accept the answers. To anticipate the outcome. To express who you are. You discovered the vast resources you have inside to conquer anything that comes your way. And now you know that the biggest struggle, the main source of stress did not come from some outside source but from your own insecurities and fears.

Embrace your new self-image. Hopefully you discovered, during quiet times, that you like who you are. That it's alright to be good to yourself. Let me share these inspirational words someone once told me: "Relax...you're already perfect."

Be Good to Yourself—You Deserve It

You know, there is something to that saying, "Today is the first day of the rest of your life. Yesterday is the past, tomorrow is the future, but today, the present, is a gift to enjoy." No doubt, you are beginning to appreciate that each day can be a brand-new start. And that the world won't come to an end if you let things go for a day.

You've just taken a transforming journey of renewal for your mind, body and spirit. A soul-stirring journey learning to express who you are. And you've spent a twenty-four-hour getaway, finding your own serene spaces—finding your quiet joy. The question now is, "What are you going to do tomorrow? What will you do with your next twenty-four hours?"

Give yourself this gift—small acts of self-nurturing; doing something that makes your happy each and every day. Make a commitment to periodically select an activity from your "wish list." Plan to escape, to take a day away once a week, once a month, twice a year. Whichever way you can fit it into your schedule. Just do it…often.

Promise to take time off for yourself again…soon.

Share Your Story:

Do you have a triumphant story of how you overcame a stressful challenge in your life? Whether from the resources in *When You Need a Timeout* or some other source, if you'd like to share your story, we'd love to hear from you. Spread hope and inspire others. Join our blog at www.thecalmingbreath.blogspot.com .

TOMORROW

About The Author

BARBARA MITCHELL is a Doctor of Clinical Hypnotherapy, Certified Stress Management Consultant and Certified Practitioner of Neuro Linguistic Programming. She is past President and Co-founder of Creative Escapes Inc., a company that specialized in sponsoring stress-management retreats for women. The two founders collaborated on writing *The Gentle Art of Relaxing With Creative Escapes*, a relaxation tape produced for Creative Escapes Inc. During this exciting period of being at the forefront of sponsoring "getaway retreats," Dr. Barbara observed how much these "escapes" improved the lives and outlook of the attendees. Their feedback and testimonials confirmed her conclusion.

After ten years in the business, Dr. Barbara desired to do more one-on-one interventions to reduce and eliminate stress-related emotional and physical problems. Subsequently, she studied cutting-edge therapeutic techniques that encompassed her multi-disciplinary background. As a result she is able to help clients achieve the desired outcome quickly and effectively.

Dr. Barbara Mitchell and her husband, Frederick Mitchell, a Reiki Master, have a private practice in Piscataway, New Jersey. She is a member of **ABH, IMDHA, IACT, ABNLP and TLTA**.